Simply Big B

Timeless Songs from the '20s, '30s and '40s

Arranged by Bernadine Johnson

Simply Big Band is a collection of classic hits from the golden age of American popular music. These songs have been carefully selected and arranged by Bernadine Johnson for Easy Piano, making them accessible to pianists of all ages. Phrase markings, articulations, fingering, pedaling and dynamics have been included to aid with interpretation, and a large print size makes the notation easy to read.

Big Band music, born in the dance and cabaret halls of the 1920s, survived the Great Depression and Prohibition, and continued entertaining audiences through the 1940s. During those years, Americans were craving new pleasures and forms of self-expression, eager to shed the previous century's Victorian virtues of emotional constraint and repression. Jazz and dancing were the perfect outlet. Big bands usually consisted of 10 to 15 instrumentalists, mostly brass and woodwind players. Some ensembles performed fully arranged music, and others relied on elaborate improvisations by soloists. These bands were led by some of America's most famous musicians, including Benny Goodman, Duke Ellington, and Count Basie, to name a few. The Big Band era was the heyday of swing—the rhythmic style of playing eighth notes in a long-short pattern. These rhythms, which kept dancers on their feet in the 1930s and 1940s, are still a pleasure to play on the piano today. Additionally, big band music also contains some of the world's greatest melodies. For these reasons and more, the music on the following pages is exciting to explore.

After all, this is *Simply Big Band!*

This book is dedicated with love to Arlene Pugno—the original "Satin Doll."
– Bernadine Johnson

Contents

As Time Goes By

Words and Music by Herman Hupfeld
Arranged by Bernadine Johnson

Bewitched, Bothered and Bewildered

Words by Lorenz Hart
Music by Richard Rodgers
Arranged by Bernadine Johnson

Blue Moon

Music by Richard Rodgers
Lyrics by Lorenz Hart
Arranged by Bernadine Johnson

Bye Bye Blackbird

Words by Mort Dixon
Music by Ray Henderson
Arranged by Bernadine Johnson

Slowly, with expression

Don't Get Around Much Anymore

Music by Duke Ellington
Lyrics by Bob Russell
Arranged by Bernadine Johnson

Chattanooga Choo Choo

Music by Harry Warren
Lyrics by Mack Gordon
Arranged by Bernadine Johnson

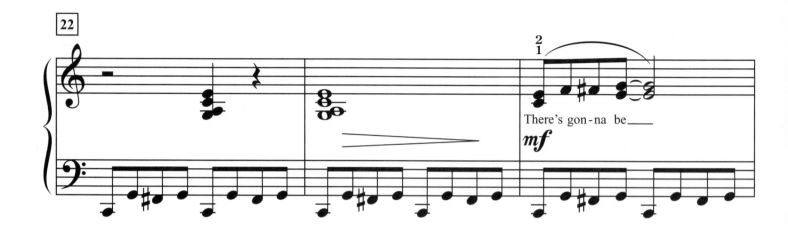

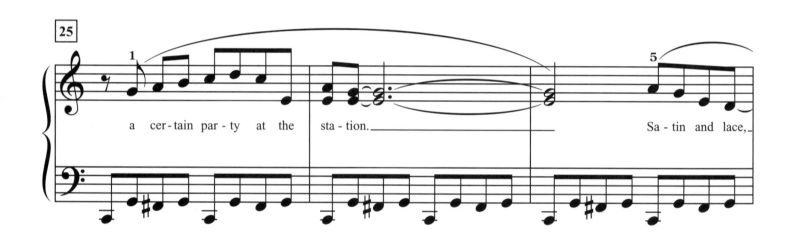

She's gon - na cry____ un - til I tell her that I'll

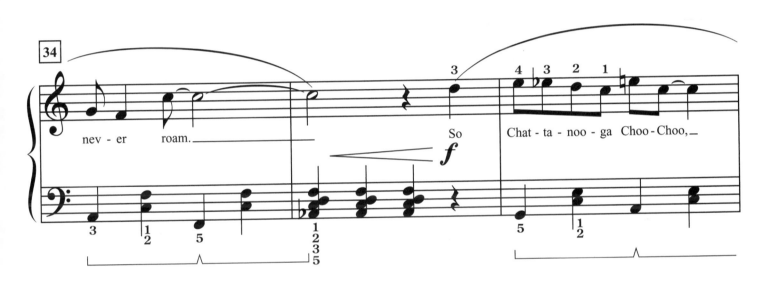

nev - er roam.____ So Chat - ta - noo - ga Choo - Choo,____

won't you choo - choo me home.

Don't Sit Under the Apple Tree

(with Anyone Else but Me)

Words and Music by
Charlie Tobias, Lew Brown and Sam H. Stept
Arranged by Bernadine Johnson

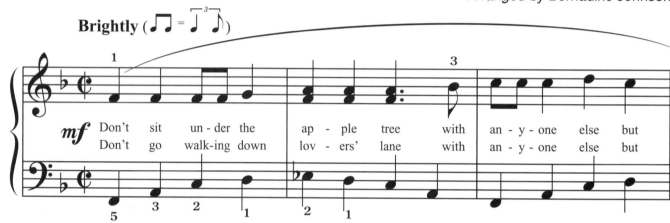

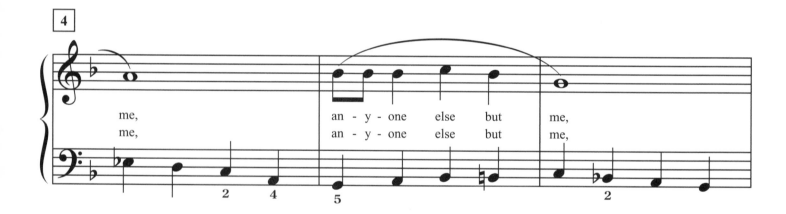

Embraceable You

Music and Lyrics by
George Gershwin and Ira Gershwin
Arranged by Bernadine Johnson

Very slowly

Five Foot Two, Eyes of Blue

Lyrics by Sam Lewis and Joe Young
Music by Ray Henderson
Arranged by Bernadine Johnson

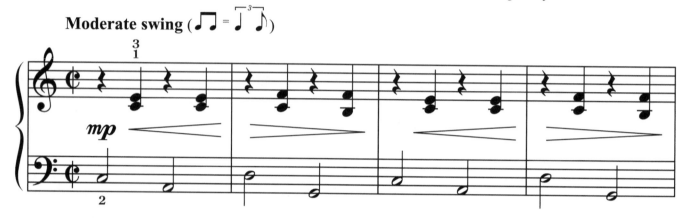

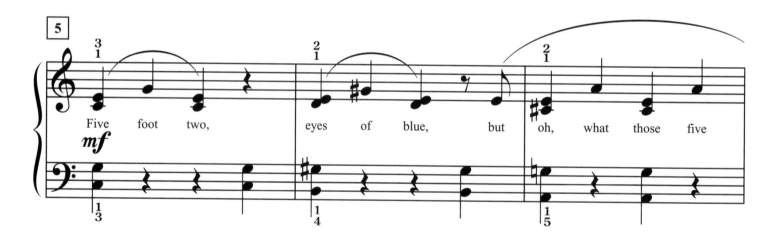

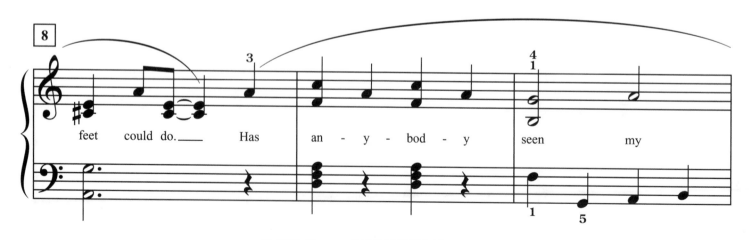

I'll Be Seeing You

Lyrics by Irving Kahal
Music by Sammy Fain
Arranged by Bernadine Johnson

Slowly, with expression

ev - 'ry - thing that's light and gay, I'll al - ways think of

cresc.

you that way. I'll find you in the morn - ing sun. And

mf

when the night is new I'll be look-ing at the moon,

a tempo

rit. *mp*

___ but I'll be see - ing you! ___

rit.

p

8va

I'm Getting Sentimental Over You

Words by Ned Washington
Music by George Bassman
Arranged by Bernadine Johnson

all I'm think-ing of. Won't you please be kind, and

just make up your mind that you'll be___ sweet and

gen-tle,___ be gen-tle with me___ be -

cause I'm___ sen-ti-men-tal___ o-ver you.

8va

In the Still of the Night

Words and Music by Cole Porter
Arranged by Bernadine Johnson

With a relaxed, "tropical" feel

It Don't Mean a Thing
(If It Ain't Got That Swing)

Music by Duke Ellington
Words by Irving Mills
Arranged by Bernadine Johnson

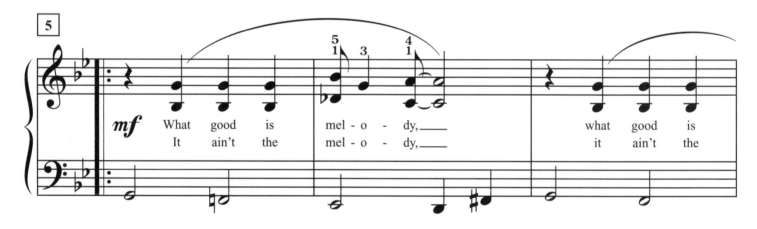

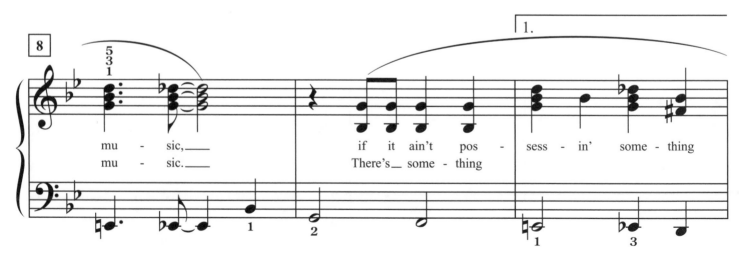

Moonglow

Words and Music by
Will Hudson, Eddie DeLange and Irving Mills
Arranged by Bernadine Johnson

My Funny Valentine

Words by Lorenz Hart
Music by Richard Rodgers
Arranged by Bernadine Johnson

Moonlight Serenade

Music by Glenn Miller
Lyrics by Mitchell Parish
Arranged by Bernadine Johnson

Moderately

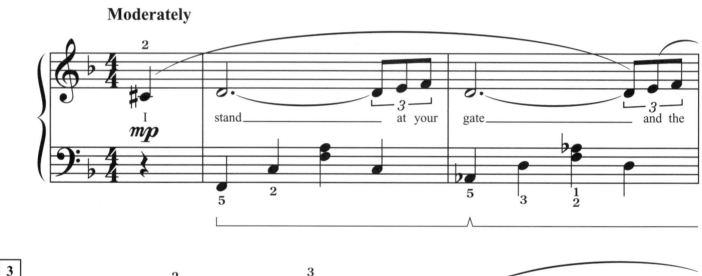

Opus One

Words and Music by
Sy Oliver and Sig Garris
Arranged by Bernadine Johnson

Satin Doll

Words and Music by
Johnny Mercer, Duke Ellington and Billy Strayhorn
Arranged by Bernadine Johnson

she digs me.
you're flip - pin'.

Out cat - tin'
Speaks La - tin

that sat - in doll..
that sat - in doll..

She's no - bod - y's fool, so I'm

play - ing it cool as can be.

I'll

Star Dust

Music by Hoagy Carmichael
Words by Mitchell Parish
Arranged by Bernadine Johnson

Stompin' at the Savoy

Lyrics by Andy Razaf
Music by Benny Goodman, Chick Webb and Edgar Sampson
Arranged by Bernadine Johnson

A String of Pearls

Music by Jerry Gray
Words by Eddie DeLange
Arranged by Bernadine Johnson

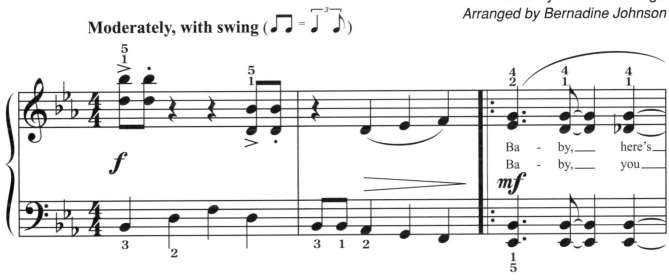

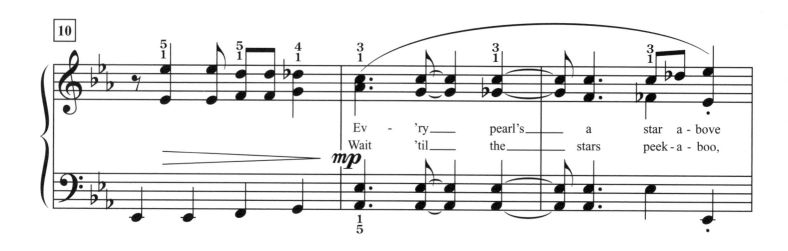

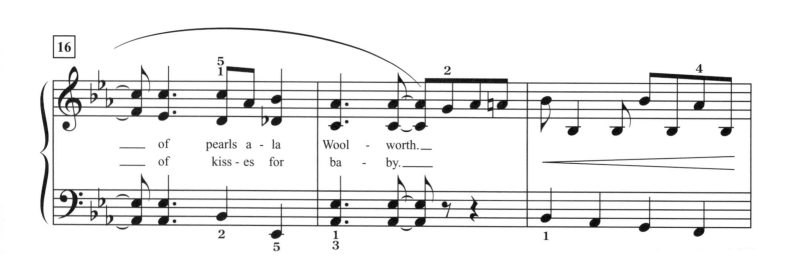

'Til that__ hap - py day in spring when you__ buy__
I found__ a__ love so sub-lime, right in__ that__

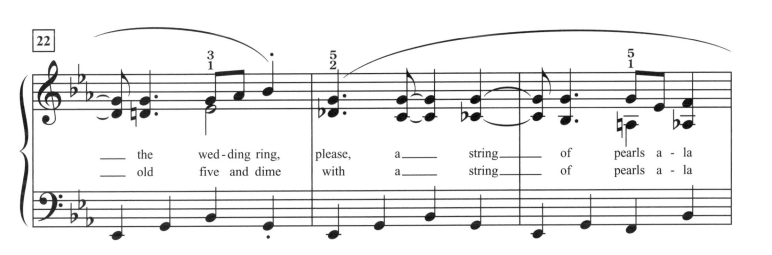

__ the wed-ding ring, please, a__ string__ of pearls a - la
__ old five and dime with a__ string__ of pearls a - la

1.
Wool - worth.__

2.
Wool - worth.__

f

8va

Sunrise Serenade

Music by Frankie Carle
Words by Jack Lawrence
Arranged by Bernadine Johnson

Look at the grass, silver in the sun, heav-y with the dew.

Look at the buds you can al-most see how they're break-in' thru.

Look at the birds feed-in' all their young in the sy-ca-mores.

But you bet-ter get on with your morn-in'

Take the "A" Train

Music and Lyrics by Billy Strayhorn
and The Delta Rhythm Boys
Arranged by Bernadine Johnson

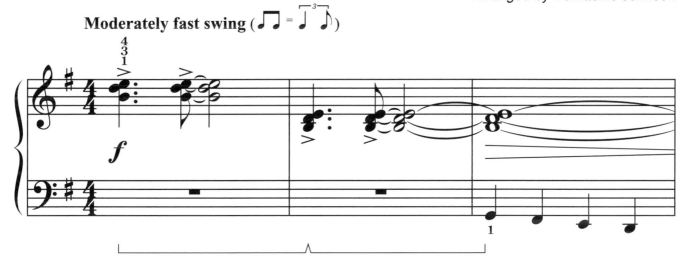

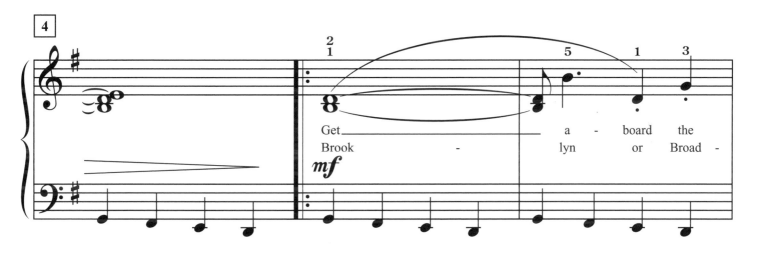

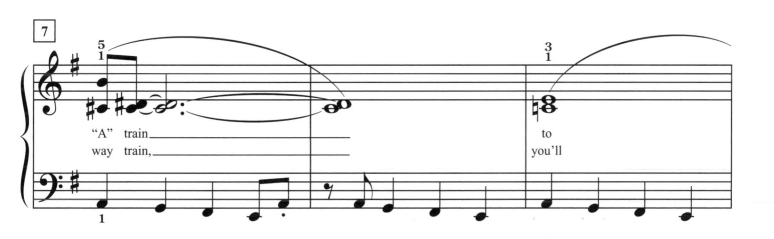

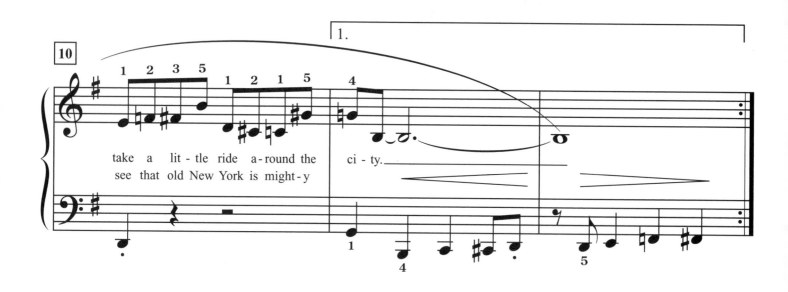

take a   lit - tle ride a - round the   ci - ty._____
see that old New York is might - y

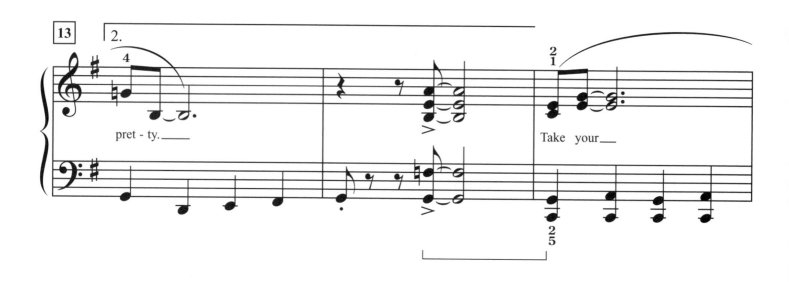

pret - ty._____   Take your___

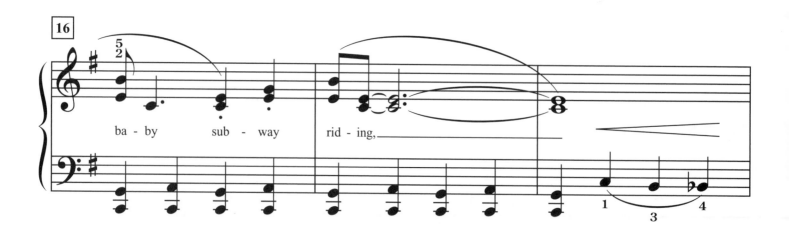

ba - by   sub - way   rid - ing,_____

They Can't Take That Away from Me

Music and Lyrics by
George Gershwin and Ira Gershwin
Arranged by Bernadine Johnson